Creative and engaging, the prom _
Micro-Moments are sure to spark the most wonderful of conversations—sometimes silly, sometimes serious, but always thoughtful and memory-making. These simple yet meaningful moments shared between mother and child will not only deepen their bond but will also lay the foundation for a lifelong love of God. Perfect for bedtime tuck-ins!

—Tama Fortner, ECPA award-winning and bestselling author of more than sixty books

Moms will love this fun book of 35 activities with fresh interactions for moms and children that will build stronger bonds. From silly and tender moments to ones that foster a child's curiosity and creativity, these fun pages will also inspire a child's development, small motor coordination, and emotional growth. The book also includes many prayers for moms to talk to God about their child.

—Karen Whiting, multi-book award-winning author, writing coach, international speaker

Mommy and Me Micro-Moments by Bitsy Kemper is a precious way to connect with your child and make memories that will last a lifetime. Whether you're a busy family on the go, or have all the time in the world, you'll end up with a keepsake to treasure as your little ones grow up.

—Joanna Rowland, author of *The Memory Box* and *Always Mom, Forever Dad*

One of the greatest gifts we moms share with our children is the passing along of our faith. In turn, our children teach us something every day about the gift of God's bountiful love. With *Mommy and Me Micro-Moments*, author and mother Bitsy Kemper provides families with a beautiful template to create a powerful season of spirituality in their homes. Packed with ideas that can be adapted for many ages and stages, this resource offers moms a wonderful, doable, enjoyable way to bring faith to life each day.

—Lisa M. Hendey, Founder of CatholicMom.com

Children start understanding life from their parents. If a parent shows an intimate relationship with God, the child will more easily grasp the concept of God. By seeing Mom mirroring God with this devotional, the child has the chance to see God Himself. Bitsy's book *Mommy &Me Micro-Moments* offers moms the power to convey that concept of our loving God, showing that God is love, allowing the child to carry a positive connection throughout their life.

—Monsignor James C. Kidder

If you're in need of a good book, I have a recommendation for you! A five-week devo by Bitsy Kemper for moms + kids to do together: *Mommy &Me Micro-Moments."*

—Stephanie Clarisse, *500 Seconds to Joy* and podcaster

Bitsy Kemper

5-MINUTE DEVOTIONAL ACTIVITIES FOR MOMS AND KIDS

mommy & me
MICRO-MOMENTS

MOMMY & ME MICRO-MOMENTS

Five Minute Devotional Fun For Busy
Moms and Kids

Bitsy Kemper

Bold Vision Books
PO Box 2011
Friendswood, TX 77549

Dedication

To moms everywhere doing their best.

We can't stop time
but we can treasure
what we have
while we have it.

God bless us, everyone.

Table of Contents

A Note from Bitsy   11

How to Use This Book   13

Day 1 Silly Moments: 1,2,3 Guess With Me   15

Day 2 Crayon Moments: In the Palm of My Hand   18

Day 3 Ask Me Moments: Colors of My Home   21

Day 4 Tender Moments: When I Grow Up   24

Day 5 Crayon Moments: Well, Look at That   27

Day 6 Ask Me Moments: People Around Me   30

Day 7 Silly Moments: Shadows of Love   32

Day 8 Tender Moments: Being Kind   34

Day 9 Ask Me Moments: Sizing Me Up   36

Day 10 Crayon Moments: Think Happy Thoughts   38

Day 11 Tender Moments: Let Me Count the Ways   41

Day 12 Silly Moments: It's a Stretch   95

Day 13 Tender Moments: Seeing With New Eyes   48

Day 14 Ask Me Moments: Today's Ordinary Specifics   50

Day 15 Silly Moments: Don't Make Me Laugh   53

Day 16 Crayon Moments: Transcribing the Day   56

Day 17 Silly Moments: Faith-based Laughs   59

Day 18 Ask Me Moments: Modern Media and Me   63

Day 19 Silly Moments: Back Talk   66

Day 20 Crayon Moments: Say Cheese   68

Day 21 Ask Me Moments: Today Will Be a Good Old Day   71

Day 22 Crayon Moments: Talk About Pop Music   74

Day 23 Silly Moments: Silly Mommy Says   76

Day 24 Crayon Moments: Branches of the Family Tree   79

Day 25 Tender Moments: Pick a Number   84

Day 26 Silly Moments: I Have to Hand it to You   87

Day 27 Tender Moments: Unconditionally 89

Day 28 Ask Me Moments: Current Faves 92

Day 29 Crayon Moments: Draw What You Hear 94

Day 30 Silly Moments: Walk This Way 99

Day 31 Tender Moments: Goodnight and God Bless 103

Day 32 Ask Me Moments: Enjoying Ourselves 106

Day 33 Tender Moments: Listen to This! 109

Day 34 Crayon Moments: Keep in Touch 112

Day 35 Ask Me Moments: At This Closing Moment 116

Where To Go From Here 120

Pressing Needs Prayers 124

Acknowledgments 135

Meet the Author 137

Scripture Index 138

A Note from Bitsy

Hey there, Mom. I am so excited for you to spend these precious weeks with your child. You already know they only stay little for so long. Wasn't it just yesterday we were bringing them home from the hospital? This book is a tangible way to capture and honor childhood moments that would otherwise go unnoticed, uncovered, or forgotten.

Since you'll be completing this book together, it's an easy way to sneak in dedicated, quality time. I mean, *any* busy mom can find five minutes a day. That's all it'll take! In that short time you'll work prayer and gratitude into daily life, allowing your child to embrace the love of God early on, and cement a lasting relationship.

If you've skimmed through the book already, you'll see this isn't your typical devotional of reading a Bible verse, saying a prayer, and reflecting. That format works great for moms, but not so much for kiddos. As a mom of three kids in four years, and a children's book author, I know how hectic life can get, and how hard it is to keep the attention span of a youngster. And, it's fun—for both of you!

To be honest, it's the devotional I wish I had when my teens were young. I mean, we all have intentions of sitting down with our child to play blocks, read bedtime stories, and even say bedtime prayers together, but unless we block out that time in ink, real life has a way of bulldozing our good intentions. It happens to all of us. With this book, you're making quality *mommy and me* time happen. It's a daily, promised time slot you are setting aside for you and your child. You'll both have this special time to look forward to before bed, or in the morning, or after work/school.

I think of St. Therese of Lisieux, after whom Mother Teresa modeled her life. Focusing on the *little way* is how they both lived their lives. They had a very basic approach—do ordinary tasks with extraordinary love. I ask you simply to do the same. If all you have is five minutes to spend with your little one, commit and make them the best five minutes of your day.

—Bitsy

How to Use This Book:

So, how does it work? Every night over 35 fun-filled days, you'll have five minutes of focused, shared time—or what I call *micro-moments*. You'll read and do each entry together. The devotionals are written to be read directly to the child by you. Some are super short and some might take the entire five minutes. Some you might choose to linger on and spend more time connecting—it's your time, you choose. All entries are interactive and enjoyable.

The simple format consists of four sections: a Bible quote, a bonding activity, a short prayer, plus a prayer of gratitude just for mom. The activities are mostly written to be done from the comfort of the child's room as you tuck them into bed. It doesn't matter when or where though—just find those five minutes each day!

There are four different bonding activity themes:

- Silly Moments: where you share a laugh
- Crayon Moments: where you capture *now* memories in your child's own hand
- Ask Me Moments: simple fill-in-the blanks to detail a personalized snapshot in time
- Tender Moments: a chance to snuggle up, talk, and reflect

In the back, I've added a list of *emergency prayers*. These are for times when your child needs specific encouragement or help and you're not sure where to turn. You can flip to the "Pressing Needs Prayers" section at any time and they'll direct you back to a related devotional day or bible verse you can reference to dig even deeper. You may never need them at all and that's fine, too.

By the end of these 35 short shared devotionals, you'll have grown in four ways:

- Your relationship with your child will deepen.
- Your relationship to God will strengthen.
- Your child's relationship to God will blossom.
- The relationship with God that you and your child now share together will become even stronger—a bond to last a lifetime.

What a wonderful gift of time to offer your child and yourself. I think of you when I see these verses:

When she speaks, her words are wise, and kindness is the rule for everything she says …. Her children stand and bless her. … "There are many fine women in the world, but you are the best of them all!"

Proverbs 31:26-29 TLB

May every moment you spend here be blessed.

DAY 1

SILLY MOMENTS:
SHARE A LAUGH

LORD, even before I say a word, you already know what I am going to say.

Psalm 139:4 ICB

1, 2, 3 Guess With Me

Mom: Read all instructions before starting!

Step 1: Both mom and child think of a food, but don't say it yet. On the count of three, say the food out loud at the same time, and see if you are both thinking the exact same food. "One, two, three ...(food)"

Hey Mom, here's the bonus part: after the count of three the first time, instead of saying a food, say MONKEY! Guaranteed laughs.

Step 2: Tell the child you got confused and you're going to try again. Now you're going to think of an animal, and on the count of three, you'll both say it out loud. "One, two, three ...(animal)."

OK, Mom, bonus time again: Odds are your child will say monkey. But you are going to say the name of the food your child just said out loud in #1. More laughs.

Step 3: Last round. Now tell your child that you're going to be serious, and on the count of three, you both are going to say who your favorite person in the room is.

Get ready, Mom. Odds are your child will say you and will expect you to say them. So, this time, on the count of three, point to yourself and say, "Me!" Haha. Smother with love and let them know you are just kidding, that they are your most favorite person. Bonus points if you can work in that they are God's favorite person too.

Dear God,

You always know what's in my heart. Before I even ask, you know me well enough to understand what I want and need. Thank you for keeping me in your loving care. Amen.

Silent Prayer of Gratitude for Mom:

Dear Lord, I know my child well and can often predict what they are going to do or say. But as much as I might want to, I can't actually read their mind. As a mom, I can feel lost when they need help, and I can't figure out how to give it to them. It's frustrating. When that happens, help me remember to take a deep breath and turn to you for guidance. Like James 1:5 says, all I need to do is ask for wisdom and you will give it to me generously. Thank you for being my hotline. Amen.

DAY 2

CRAYON MOMENTS:
GET CREATIVE

See, I have written your name on my hand. ... Look up and look around you. All your children are gathering to return to you.

Isaiah 49:16,18 ICB

In The Palm of My Hand

**Mom: Draw an outline of your hand. Then, with a different color, draw an outline of your child's hand nestled inside it. Snap a picture with your phone of the keepsake to treasure whenever you need a pick-me-up. **

Dear Future Me,

My hand looks so small compared to Mommy's. Someday, when I look back at this drawing and press my hand against it to see how I have grown, I will think of the image of God holding all of us in the palm of his hand. He holds us close and keeps us safe. Just like how I keep growing, God's love never stops growing for us. May our love for *him* continue to grow too.

Silent Prayer of Gratitude for Mom:

Dear Lord, As I look at this little hand of my child compared to mine, I see how small they are. Yet when I think back to when they were born, and how tiny they were then, their little hand today seems so big in comparison. To think it will someday grow to be the size of mine, or even bigger. Thank you for this amazing gift of a child, growing every day not only in size, but in your love. Amen.

DAY 3

ASK ME MOMENTS: CAPTURING THE DAYS

The decorations were green, white, and blue, fastened with purple ribbons tied to silver rings imbedded in marble pillars. Gold and silver benches stood on pavements of black, red, white, and yellow marble.

Esther 1:6 TLB

Colors of My Home

Let's take a few minutes to capture a few colorful details of this childhood home.

My bedroom walls are the color(s) _____

The blanket and sheets I'm using right now are the color _____
and have a design that looks like _____

The inside of our home is mostly the color _____

Appliances in our kitchen are the color _____

Our floors are mainly the color _____

My favorite color is _____

Dear Lord,

Our lives are filled with colors and wonder. Seasons change and paint colors fade, but we know your love for us never fades. We are blessed to be surrounded by your colorful glory. Amen.

Silent Prayer of Gratitude for Mom:

God, I know I am doing your will, but I'll be honest in saying not all days are sunshine and rainbows. It feels like there are so many ways to mess up parenting responsibilities. Yet, I yearn to do what's right so I can see the vivid colors of your glory, face to face. I can only do that with your help. Bless me with the many shades of love. Amen.

DAY 4

TENDER MOMENTS:
SHARE YOUR HEART

*So encourage each other to build each other up, just as you are
already doing.*

1 Thessalonians 5:11 TLB

When I Grow Up

While snuggling next to your young one, ask what they want to be when
they grow up. Write it here:

_____

_____

_____

_____

Gently ask for details, like why they want to be that, how they thought of it, and what they think their job responsibilities will be. There are no wrong answers; have an easy conversation. No matter what they say, praise and encourage them. Call out skill sets they have now that would make them good at what they want to be. Be specific, concrete, honest, and optimistic. Say phrases such as:

> "You have such great patience. You'll be a wonderful pet trainer."

> "You are so good at solving puzzles. You will be a great detective."

> "You love learning about planets. I bet you'll have so much fun as an astronaut."

Foster their young dreams and sense of adventure.

Dear Jesus,

I may be small, but I can do anything I put my mind to try. Encourage me to keep growing and learning. When I am big and strong, remind me to give you credit for all my blessings. Amen.

Silent Prayer of Gratitude for Mom:

> Dear Jesus, There are times I look around and marvel that *I'm* the grown-up. I don't always feel qualified. Imagining this little person beside me becoming someone my age almost makes me laugh. How lucky I am to play a role in their growth. It's

encouraging to know you trust me so much that you've chosen me as the person to raise them here on earth. I am blessed with this gift of mommyhood. Amen.

DAY 5

CRAYON MOMENTS: GET CREATIVE

The heavens tell the glory of God. And the skies announce what his hands have made.

Psalm 19:1 ICB

Well, Look at That

Look out the window closest to you. Ask your child what they see. It is light or dark out? Do they see the sun, clouds, moon, or stars? Has there been rain making the ground wet? Are there trees or streets? Flowers? People? Animals? Draw what you see. Then, together, describe and write in words what you've drawn.

Note to Mom: this isn't just drawing fun. By asking them to describe what they see, you get to see and experience the world through their eyes. It also captures a moment in time; this view won't look the same in a year, or five, or ten—just like your child, it may even be a little bit different tomorrow.

Dear Lord,

You made the skies and the world. Just like you sent sun for plants to live, you sent your Son for us to live—forever. Then you gave us the Holy Spirit, making you a holy three-in-one. We might not be able to see or touch a wonder like the Holy Trinity with our eyes or hands, but we can feel it in our hearts. Just like the heavens and sky, we too proclaim your glory. Amen.

Silent Prayer of Gratitude for Mom:

Dear Lord, Psalm 19:1 says the heavens declare your glory, and the skies proclaim your handiwork. While I might not shout your name in the streets or off rooftops, I see and am in awe of your great works. Today I have a simple prayer of gratitude—thank you for all you've given us. Amen.

DAY 6

ASK ME MOMENTS: CAPTURING THE DAYS

And good advice from a friend is sweet.

Proverbs 27:9 ICB

People Around Me

Let's capture some social moments in time.

The coolest person ever is _____

My best friends are _____

If I wanted to do something nice for my friend or friends, I could

_____

My last playdate, or time I went to a park, was on _____

with _____

My most recent birthday party theme was _____

When I'm with friends, I like to _____

Dear Jesus,

Help me to be the kind of person I admire—kind, honest, and generous. Help me be the kind of friend you were to your best friends, and to everyone you met. Amen.

Silent Prayer of Gratitude for Mom:

> Jesus, Today we read that a person's sweet words to a friend make the heart glad. May I cherish all the sweet words spoken to me. May I speak more sweet words to my friends and family. Who doesn't like making the heart glad? Amen.

DAY 7

SILLY MOMENTS
SHARE A LAUGH

All good giving and every perfect gift is from above, coming down from the Father of lights, with whom there is no alteration or shadow caused by change.

James 1:17 NABRE

Shadows of Love

Mom: While I definitely advocate being in the moment and putting away your phone, tonight we are putting your phone to good use.

1. If desired, do an internet search for "how to make shadow puppets with hands" videos and pick one to watch together. Otherwise, get ready to go rogue and experiment with making your own.
2. Decide whether you want to make shadow puppets on the wall or on the ceiling.

3. Turn on your phone's flashlight and dim or turn off the room lights. You'll be taking turns holding the phone. One of you will shine the flashlight as the other makes and projects the shadow puppets. Then, it's the other person's turn to make shadow puppets.

How fun is that? You now have something to do together at hotels, at family gatherings, etc. As your child grows, they'll be able to share this party trick at sleepovers—and be thinking of you the whole time.

Dear Lord,

Thank you for the gift of art and illusion. It's so fun to be creative. We know there are no shadow tricks when it comes to following your path, though. The truth is never an illusion. Remind me to turn to prayer whenever I need help in seeing real from fake, right from wrong. With the time Mommy and I have spent together so far, I really like seeing the many ways we can be creatively prayerful together. Thanks for showing me I can choose fun *and* faith. Amen.

Silent Prayer of Gratitude for Mom:

> Even in the shadows, Lord, your light is lit within me. My child is a perfect gift, come down from above, from the Father of light. Help me let this little light of mine shine in your glory. Amen.

DAY 8

TENDER MOMENTS: SHARE YOUR HEART

And if, as my representatives, you give even a cup of cold water to a little child, you will surely be rewarded.

Matthew 10:42 TLB

Being Kind

Mom: As you get ready for bed, ask your child if they can think of a time when they were extra kind or helpful. Maybe they gave away something significant because they knew it would mean even more to someone else. Maybe they helped with a food drive for people in need. Maybe they took extra care to hand-make someone a special Christmas gift or birthday card. Ask them if they know that there were times they were kind and they didn't even realize it! Kindness is picking up something the teacher dropped or hugging a sad friend to make them feel better. It is smiling at someone at the grocery store. Kindness is sitting next to someone at the playground, or helping them up the slide. Even the smallest acts of kindness can make a big impact. Every action holds the same amount of weight to God, whether it's a well-planned-out huge act or a small one done with love. Remind them that simply offering someone a glass of water when they are thirsty makes God happy.

Dear Lord,

Doing little acts of kindness isn't very hard. Tomorrow, let me think of small ways to be extra helpful. Let me do them in your name. It will make me happy, the person I'm helping happy, and most importantly, it will make you happy. Amen.

Silent Prayer of Gratitude for Mom:

> Those past bedtime "Mom, I need a glass of water." interruptions? Those "I forgot to tell you I need 35 cupcakes for scouts this afternoon" statements? Those "MOOOOM! I CAN'T FIND MY SHOES" when child is standing in front of the door where said shoes are staring them in the face moments? Jesus, I need you by my side at every one of them. As moms, completing these small acts of kindness (OK, service) feel like they never end. Dear Lord, help me remember that any and all tasks done for our child are never lost in God's eyes. How lucky we are to have someone that needs us, to have someone to care for. Help me remember we are tending to God in the process. Amen.

DAY 9

ASK ME MOMENTS: CAPTURING THE DAYS

But I am like an olive tree growing in God's Temple. I trust God's love forever and ever.

Psalm 52:8 ICB

Sizing Me Up

I am about _____ feet, _____ inches tall.

I weigh _____ pounds.

I wear a size _____ shoe.

I wear size _____ clothes.

My favorite piece of clothing is _____

The last time I wore a hat was _____

for _____

There is NO WAY I will wear _____

Dear God,

You love me no matter how I grow, what I wear, or what I look like. Mommy does too. Thank you for giving me such a faith-filled parent that shows me how deep your love for me is. Amen.

Silent Prayer of Gratitude for Mom:

> Jesus, It feels like time keeps speeding up. I want to hold on to these precious young moments and never let them go, but I know I need to make room for my child, and myself, and our relationship, to grow. Thank you for being here every step of the way. Amen.

DAY 10

CRAYON MOMENTS:
GET CREATIVE

Be very careful what you think. Your thoughts run your life.

Proverbs 4:23 ICB

Think Happy Thoughts

Mom: Say to your child, "Think about people, places, and things that make you happy. Let's draw one of them." Maybe it's a Ferris wheel, snack, sport activity, or group of people.

Talk about these happy things while you're drawing. Ask questions such as:

- What about it makes you so happy?
- When you think of it, does it make you smile?
- Are there ways you can spend more time thinking those happy thoughts?

Isn't this great insight? It's also helpful to know these things when trying to cheer your child up or distract them. You can bring up the things they mentioned, and make them smile.

Alternatively, instead of talking, you can choose to enjoy quiet time together while drawing, playing soft music in a calming, dimly-lit room. Take cues from your child on which one they need today.

Dear Jesus,

Thinking happy thoughts makes me happy. What we think about most decides where we go and what we do. Help keep our minds focused on the positive. We are grateful you can help steer us to joy, and that you continue to shower us with joy. Amen.

Silent Prayer of Gratitude for Mom:

Jesus, Oh, how easy it is to get caught up in "stinkin' thinkin'." When bad moods roll in like clouds on a rainy day, it can be hard to shift out of that gloomy mindset. Help me remember Proverbs 4:23. Help me remember that my thoughts affect my actions. If I can't shake the bad mood at the time, help curb any negative actions or reactions that might be tempted to result from it. If I can remember my child smiling about what they talked about today, I'm bound to start smiling too, and release negativity. Amen.

DAY 11

TENDER MOMENTS: SHARE YOUR HEART

I give you a new commandment: love one another. As I have loved you, so you also should love one another.

John 13:34 NABRE

Let Me Count the Ways

Share 5 specific attributes you love about each other. That's it.

Child, I love these qualities about you:

4.

5.

Mom, I love this about you:

1.

2.

3.

4.

5.

Dear Lord,

These five items we have listed are but a fraction of the ways our family loves each other. If life gets thorny or if we ever need reminding, we can come back to this page and refresh our memories. Like your love for us, this kind of love never fades. Amen.

Silent Prayer of Gratitude for Mom:

Dear Jesus, If all we must do is love each other, then I think we have fulfilled the law. OK, sure, we might have our moments of discord, but love is always there. Just like your love is always present. Amen.

DAY 12

SILLY MOMENTS: SHARE A LAUGH

Trust the LORD with all your heart. Don't depend on your own understanding.

Proverbs 3:5 ICB

It's a Stretch

As you're winding down tonight with this journal, tell your child you're going to do some bedtime stretches together. But, pssst, Mom, read all instructions before starting.

Step 1: Have your child lean over and touch their toes as best as they can. You do it with them, whether you're sitting alongside, or in a chair.

<u>Step 2:</u> Next, sit up straight. Together, slowly turn your heads to the left, and to the right. Roll shoulders backward, then forward, then backward.

<u>Step 3:</u> Now say to reach up high and stretch tall.

Mom, this is the fun part: when your child is reaching, swoop in for a tickle party. They'll never see it coming. Haha.

Dear Future Me,

Sometimes results turn out differently than we expect. But don't forget, God is on our side. Trust that he will make it all work out right.

Silent Prayer of Gratitude for Mom:

Dear God, Parenting is hard. There is plenty I don't understand. I have faith that I'm doing my best, and I can only do that by trusting your understanding is far greater than mine. Jesus, I trust in you. Amen.

Day 13

TENDER MOMENTS: SHARE YOUR HEART

No one can really know what anyone else is thinking or what he is really like except that person himself. ...And God has actually given us his Spirit (not the world's spirit) to tell us about the wonderful free gifts of grace and blessing that God has given us.

1 Corinthians 2:11-12 TLB

Seeing With New Eyes

Snuggle time. Get in close with your loved one, whether you put your arm around them as you lie next to them, or you face each other. Ask them if anything is bothering them. You will only really know if you ask. (You might think you know what is going on in their little mind, but when you open the door for them to talk to you, you might get a completely different reply.) The point of today isn't to bring the mood down. The point isn't to solve the problem. Tonight is to look at whatever might be going on in their mind or world with new eyes. If someone is not being nice to them—maybe that person has a tough time at home and isn't nice to anyone right now. Are they concerned about the upcoming school year? Suggest they focus on the summer days ahead instead. End with a hug and a promise that you are always there to talk with them.

Dear Future Me.

Mom cares so very much. She is there to help, to listen, to hug, or to laugh with you. Make sure you treat her with as much kindness as she has given you.

Silent Prayer of Gratitude for Mom:

> Jesus, No one can really know what is going on in another person's life. There are times I have no idea what's going on in my child's head. Through your grace, I can catch my breath and do my best to see the moment from their perspective. It doesn't always work, I'll be honest, but asking the Holy Spirit for help in the moment sure does make a difference. Thank you for sending your Spirit when we ask. Remind me to ask more often, Amen.

DAY 14

ASK ME MOMENTS: CAPTURING THE DAYS

This the day the LORD has made; let us rejoice in it and be glad.

Psalm 118:24 NABRE

Today's Ordinary Specifics

Today we went to _____

and we _____

_____

_____

Other than family members, the people I saw today include

_____

_____

I wore a _____   _____ top and a
         (type)   (color)

_____   _____ bottom
  (type)   (color)

and _____shoes.
                  (type and color)

We ate _____ for breakfast,
               (type of food)

_____ for lunch,
               (type of food)

and _____ for dinner.
               (type of food)

My favorite part about today was

_____

_____

Dear Lord,

As days turn into weeks, weeks turn into months, and months turn into years, I am ever grateful for the simple blessings in life. Every day is perfect when we spend it with family—and you. Amen.

Silent Prayer of Gratitude for Mom:

> Dear God, You made today and everything in it. Help me find ways to rejoice and be glad no matter what went on (not all days are perfect, after all). Tomorrow, may I wake up rejoicing in a new day, knowing you made it too, full of new possibilities and opportunities. Amen.

DAY 15

SILLY MOMENTS:
SHARE A LAUGH

God did not give us a spirit that makes us afraid. He gave us a spirit of power and love and self-control.

2 Timothy 1:7 ICB

Don't Make Me Laugh

Mom: Read this, or explain in your own words: Have you had the grumpies today? Maybe yesterday or another time? Being cranky can make even fun stuff, well, less fun. How do you shake yourself out of a bad mood? It's not always easy. Grown-ups have a hard time, too. Let's practice one way to get rid of the grumpies without saying a word. You can do this anytime you or someone you know is grumpy. You can even do it on your own in a mirror.

Mom: You'll each have a turn, but you go first. No talking—but sound effects are allowed. Remind them to keep a straight face, as the goal is to not laugh. Of course, your goal is to make them giggle. Make the silliest faces you can. Add silly sounds. Maybe you make a monkey face and go HOOOH HOOH like you're trying to climb a tree. Try making a fish face by sucking in your cheeks while crossing your eyes. Move your arms like you're swimming different kinds of strokes in the pool while saying WHOOP WHOOP or SWISH SWISH SPLASH. The other person is not allowed to laugh. Keep at it, making as many faces and sounds as you need to until they cave. Then it's their turn to make you laugh. See how long you can each go before cracking up.

Dear God,

You want us to be happy. We see signs of it all around us, from the yummy taste of ice cream and treats to the cute sound of a kitten's little meow. Remind us that we might not be able to control others, or our situation, but we can always control our reaction to it. Like it says in the book of Timothy, you have given us the power of self-control. Just because we are in a bad mood doesn't mean we have to stay in a bad mood. Amen.

Silent Prayer of Gratitude for Mom:

God, A spirit of power and self-control is hard to teach. They usually need to be experienced. Yet there will be time and time again when my child needs to learn and use them. I pray I can effectively empower them to advocate for themselves. You have given us the ability to do so. Thanks for entrusting us to be strong. Amen.

DAY 16

CRAYON MOMENTS:
GET CREATIVE

If we live in the Spirit, let us also follow the Spirit.

Galatians 5:25 NABRE

Transcribing the Day

Mom: Ask your child to describe something they saw or did today, and use this space to write down what they said, word for word. Capture their tone of voice, mannerisms, and overall beauty of their age. If you'd like, you can ask what they think God was doing or thinking at the same time. Have them autograph the bottom of the page.

Dear Lord,

We may not say your name every second of every day, but we know *you* think of us, and look after us, every second of every day. How lucky we are to be under your constant care. Amen.

Silent Prayer of Gratitude for Mom:

> Jesus, I can't go wrong by keeping in step with the Spirit. But it's not always easy. Life is complicated. I, like most moms, am busy. Please help make sure I never get too busy to look up and search for your light leading my path. Amen.

DAY 17

SILLY MOMENTS:
SHARE A LAUGH

God will yet fill your mouth with laughter. And he will fill your lips with shouts of joy.

Job 8:21 ICB

Faith-based Laughs

You've been working hard, you two. You're about halfway through the journal already. I hope you're having fun. How about some (more) laughs?

Q. What nursery song did Jesus probably hear the most?

A. Mary Had a Little Lamb.

Q. Why didn't Noah catch much fish?

A. He only had two worms.

Q. Which animals did Noah refuse to play card games with?

A. Cheetahs.

Q. What type of lighting did Noah add to his boat?

A. Floodlights.

Q. What do pirates call Noah's boat?

A. An *arrrrrr*k.

Q. Why did Moses cross the Red Sea?

A. To get to the other side.

Q. What would the best names be for the Apostles' boats?

A. Wor*ship* and Disciple*ship*.

Q. Why don't sponges have to go to church?

A. They are already hole-y.

Q. Do you know where they found Solomon's temple?

A. On the side of his head.

Q. What's the best way to send a prayer to God?

A. Kneemail.

Q. What time of day was Adam created?

A. A little before Eve.

Q. What did Adam say when asked what his favorite day of the year is?

A. "It's New Years, Eve."

Q. What do we have that Adam and Eve never had?

A. Grandparents.

Q. What proof do we have that Adam was a super-fast runner?

A. He was first in the human race.

Q. What did the student say when asked why he always came in from lunch alongside the same person?

A. "I was told to walk by Faith."

Dear Jesus,

Life can be as fun as we want it to be. Happiness is a choice. May we find ways to fill our days with laughter. As we enjoy ourselves, guide our hearts and speech to always reflect your grace. Amen.

Silent Prayer of Gratitude for Mom:

> Dear Lord, Thanks for having fun with us. Sharing these giggles with my child tonight and hearing them laugh is a moment and feeling I want to continue sharing long into their adulthood. Thank you for the medicine of laughter. Amen.

DAY 18

ASK ME MOMENTS: CAPTURING THE DAYS

Sing out, heavens, and rejoice, earth, break forth into song, you mountains.

Isaiah 49:13 NABRE

Modern Media and Me

Mom: Let's capture the music and media of the moment.

The type or genre of music I like to listen to the most is

_____

The best musical I've seen or heard is

_____

A sound that makes me smile is

_____

The TV show I have the most fun watching is

_____

I love the comedy or drama movie

_____

and have watched it _____ times.

A really funny video I saw is

_____

and shows _____

The device I usually use to watch videos or listen to music is called a/an

_____

model/type _____

Dear Jesus,

Technology may change, but we never need to update you to your latest version. We never have to *subscribe* to your love. We sing out to you with joy for being the best brand name ever. Amen.

Silent Prayer of Gratitude for Mom:

> Dear God, For every moment my heart has been bursting with joy to the point I feel like breaking out in song like in a musical, thank you. For each and every occasion I have literally shouted for joy, thank you. And thank you for all the rejoicing yet to come. Amen.

DAY 19

SILLY MOMENTS: SHARE A LAUGH

One thing I do know is that I was blind and now I see.

John 9:25 NABRE

Back Talk

Mom: You get to start out lying down for this one. Stretch out on the bed, facing down. Close your eyes, or if you can stand it, place the pillow over your head so your kiddo knows you're not peeking. Ask them to pick something out in the room, and gently place it on your back. You have to guess what it is using only one hand. Bonus points if you can guess right as it's placed on your back, without ever touching it. When you guess right, it's their turn.

Dear Jesus,

Prayer and faith seem to be the only ways to "see" you, Lord. But I don't have to be able to see you in person to know how to follow you. You (and Mom) are teaching me the right path. Amen.

Silent Prayer of Gratitude for Mom:

> Dear Lord, There have been times when I've been blind to what's right there, in front (or behind or to the side) of me. It took some groping around to figure out how to see it. I was lost trying to figure out how to handle it. All I needed to do was believe. I know that faith will always lead me back to you. Amen.

DAY 20

CRAYON MOMENTS:
GET CREATIVE

It is good and pleasant when God's people live together in peace!

Psalm 133:1 ICB

Say Cheese

Mom: Have your child draw a quick family portrait of everyone that lives in your house right now. Include any pets. Add names under everyone, so you have a great keepsake.

If the two of you live alone, ask your child to draw a picture of your family, and see who they choose to include. When finished, snap a pic and text it to whomever they include. That person will be thrilled to know they are considered family.

Dear Lord,

Bless this house and everyone in it. Watch over us tonight, and keep us safe and free from harm. We thank you for your many, many gifts, and for all those yet to come. We love you, we praise you, and we hope to someday deserve you. Amen.

Silent Prayer of Gratitude for Mom:

> Jesus, How wonderful to spend these past 20 special nights together one on one, even if they last but micro-moments. I know there are nights when the whole family can be at odds. Grant me patience and wisdom at those times. Help guide me to peaceful resolutions. Psalm 133:1 is right. It is good and pleasing when we all get along. Amen.

DAY 21

ASK ME MOMENTS: CAPTURING THE DAYS

Don't long for "the good old days," for you don't know whether they were any better than these!

Ecclesiastes 7:10 TLB)

Today Will Be a Good Old Day

Mom: While these questions might initially seem superfluous and have nothing to do with capturing childhood, you and your child will look back in amazement at the world as it is today. (If you happen to know the answers from when you were young, add them in too.) Imagine the fun you'll both have looking back at the responses for the future.

The current president is

I want the next president to be:

_____

A gallon of gas costs $_____, and a 4-door sedan made by
_____ costs: $_____.

I bet by the time I can drive, gas will cost $_____ and
that kind of car will cost $_____.

Milk costs $_____ for one gallon. When I'm an adult,
I think it will cost $_____.

My last pair of shoes were for _____ and
cost $_____, which is [more/less] than
average. I think by the time I'm in high school, a typical pair like that will
cost: $_____.

A recent headline that grown-ups keep talking about is

_____

Mom would prefer the news talked more about

_____

By the time I follow the news, I bet I'll hear/watch it this way:

_____

instead of a newspaper or TV.

Dear Lord,

No matter what the future holds, all I can focus on is now. Like it says in the book of Micah, help me to act justly, love kindly, and walk humbly with you by my side. That means I want to listen and be kind to others, remember to be thankful, and ask for help when I need it. How could tomorrow be any better than today if I do all that? Amen.

Silent Prayer of Gratitude for Mom:

> Sometimes it's easy to get caught up in the past, thinking about how easy life was back then. Life is pretty hectic now. But how funny to think that I will someday look back at today as *one of the good old days*. Help me take life one day at a time. Amen.

DAY 22

CRAYON MOMENTS:
GET CREATIVE

Speak to each other with psalms, hymns, and spiritual songs.
Sing and make music in your hearts to the Lord.

Ephesians 5:19 ICB

Talk About Pop Music

Mom: Write some lyrics to a favorite or currently popular song. Maybe there's a song you've sung to them since they were a baby? Perhaps you can think of a trendy, popular jingle people repeat? Ask your child what they think of when they hear the tune. Write their words in the space provided. Discuss why the song is special or why it's an earworm. Sing a short verse together. Then share a nugget of what your parents sang to *you*, or a popular song from when you were their age.

_____

_____

_____

_____

_____

_____

_____

_____

This will be a fun memory to look back on in the future. The odds are you will long forget this trendy tune by the time you look back at this journal.

Dear God,

Singing lifts our voices to the heavens. Can you hear us? We sing for you. Amen.

Silent Prayer of Gratitude for Mom:

> Dear Jesus, No matter what trends come and go—I will sing your praises. The song may be in my heart and not come out of my lips—everyone around me might be thankful for that. But know I carry you in my heart at all times. Amen.

DAY 23

SILLY MOMENTS: SHARE A LAUGH

Carefully obey the commands I am giving you today. Love the LORD your God. Serve him with your whole being.

Deuteronomy 11:13 ICB

Silly Mommy Says

Mom: Tonight, you'll play a version of "Simon Says." In this version, it's "Silly Mommy Says." Have some fun asking them to do silly movements and actions. Anytime you trick them into doing it without saying "Silly Mommy Says" first, they have to give you a hug.

Here's a suggested script:

Silly Mommy Says stick out your tongue.

Silly Mommy Says keep your tongue out and clap your hands.

Silly Mommy Says keeping doing that and nod your head up and down.

Now shake your head from side to side. [If they move their head side to side, you didn't say "Silly Mommy Says" first, so they must hug you]

Silly Mommy Says smile.

Silly Mommy Says frown.

Silly Mommy Says make a face like you ate a pickle.

Silly Mommy Says put on your pajamas.

Come back to bed. ["Didn't say 'Silly Mommy Says.' You owe me a hug"]

Put your head on the pillow. ["Didn't say 'Silly Mommy Says.' You owe me a hug"]

If you'd like (and I'm sure they will), allow them a turn, "Silly [name of child] Says."

Dear Lord,

Help us to listen carefully to your word. It's not always easy to hear when we are in the middle of working or playing. When we *think* we are listening but not, it is easy to make mistakes. We know we are loved anyway, and no matter how many times we mess up, you are waiting there to give us a hug. Amen.

Silent Prayer of Gratitude for Mom:

God, I am doing my best to observe your commandments. I am doing my best to serve others, and by doing so, serve you. When I mess up, I appreciate your virtual hugs of forgiveness. Amen.

DAY 24

CRAYON MOMENTS: GET CREATIVE

And I will continue this agreement between us generation after generation, forever, for it shall be between me and your children as well.

Genesis 17:7 TLB

Branches of the Family Tree

Mom: Grab some crayons. Use them to chart out a family tree. Start at the bottom center, adding your child's name and any siblings. Either of you can write the names. Then draw a line straight up with your name and the child's father's name. Next to each of you, add names of any siblings (aunts/uncles). Branch off by adding two new straight lines, one above you and one above the father's name, and add the name of each of your parents (the child's grandparents). Add any siblings they may have (great aunts/uncles). Do the same for their parents (great-grandparents).

Go as far back as you can, as space or memory allows.

While you or your child are writing each name, talk about each person. Share a fond memory of each person, especially if they've never heard of that person. What a gift to offer your child a cherished memory of their historical family tree.

81

If you'd like to do some mind-boggling math, look at these numbers. For your child to be born, they needed:

- ☐ 2 parents
- ☐ 4 grandparents
- ☐ 8 great grandparents
- ☐ 16 great-great grandparents
- ☐ 32 great-great-great grandparents
- ☐ 64 great-great-great-great grandparents
- ☐ 128 great-great-great-great-great grandparents
- ☐ 256 great-great-great-great-great-great grandparents

Looking as far back as 12 previous generations, your child needed a total of 4,094 ancestors over the last 400 years!

Dear Lord,

As we look at this tree, we see we are made up of all those generations that came before us. We represent a long line of your people. May we live a life worthy of all they've sacrificed and done for us. May we continue to lead lives based on the sturdy Christian values we're building. Amen.

Silent Prayer of Gratitude for Mom:

God, As I think about my parents, grandparents, great-grandparents, and all the ancestors it took for me to get here, and for my child to get here is, incredible. Wow. To think you guided every one of them, Lord, and you're still here guiding me. I hope that with your continued help, I can live a life that makes them proud. Amen.

DAY 25

TENDER MOMENTS: SHARE YOUR HEART

Remember your creator while you are young.

Ecclesiastes 12:1 ICB

Pick a Number

Let's take some time to look back. Ask your child to pick a month of the year. Prompt them if they need reminding what months are. Next, have them pick a year between the year they were born and the current year. Depending on their age, they may need a little help—in which case, give them a choice between three numbers of your choosing (Example: "Pick year 2020, 2021, or 2022"). Let's say you've chosen May 2023.

Now grab your phone and open your photos app. In the search bar, go to the chosen month and year. (In this case, May 2023.) You'll be given a set of thumbnail photos for every pic you took for that month, in that year. What do you see? There will be places you visited, special times, and special people. Oh, such amazing memories. Hairstyles alone might be worth a laugh. Click on a few photos that call to you. Ask your child what they remember about the photo being taken. What was going on at the time? Ask for specifics. What could they hear? What could they smell? What were they thinking at that very moment? What had they recently eaten? If the photo is from when they were a tiny baby, talk to them about it. Tell them what *you* were thinking. Tell them the sounds you heard at that moment, the scent in the air, the feel of their baby soft blankets, how tiny their little feet were, and how sweet their little voice was as it cooed. What kind of baby were they at that time? Did they sleep well or did they cry all the time? Did they need mommy 24/7? What words could they say at the time? Try to remember, and share, all you can about that snapshot in time. They will love hearing about themselves. It might be the first, if not only, time they've heard these stories.

When you're ready, play the game again. Pick a new month and year. Have a glimpse at another time. How long ago does it feel for them—a long time ago? Like yesterday? What about for you?

Dear Jesus,

When I was little and too young to pray on my own, Mommy prayed for me. Now that I'm big, I get to pray for *her*. I get to pray *with* her. I'm thankful for our special prayer time together. Amen.

Silent Prayer of Gratitude for Mom:

Dear Jesus, Looking back on when our little one was even more little, I think how time goes by so fast. There were times we barely slept, let alone prayed. It makes me wonder, *Did we pay enough attention to you back then?* But I know *you* don't think that way. You don't keep score. You stick by us when we forget our bedtime prayers or forget to say grace. You know what's in our hearts. Stay with us. Let our youthfulness never be an excuse to forget or ignore our faith. In Jesus' name, amen.

DAY 26

SILLY MOMENTS: SHARE A LAUGH

You understand my thoughts from afar.

Psalm 139:2 NABRE

I Have to Hand it to You

Mom: Tonight, you're going to tell each other what you did all day, from morning until now. But here's the tricky part: you can't talk to each other. You can only communicate with gestures and hand signals. The person who is *listening* can confirm what you're saying. For example, "You had eggs for breakfast." You can also ask for clarification with a question like, "Are you talking about your friend?"

Bonus: Ask your child if you can record their telling of their day and get ready to hit that red video button on your phone—but only if they say yes. It's bound to make a great keepsake. If they say no, consider asking if you can record a few minutes, or one part. Don't pressure them though. If they decline both requests, please respect that decision.

Dear Lord,

Thank you for this connection we have between mother and child. Just like in our relationship with you, we don't need words to understand each other. Such love. What a blessing. Amen.

Silent Prayer of Gratitude for Mom:

Lord, While you know what's in my heart, I still pray. May I not be boastful about my prayer life to others. It's a personal conversation between you and me. But I do like my child seeing and hearing me pray. I love it when they *catch me in the act,* so they know prayer is a standard part of everyday life. As they see my relationship with you, it strengthens their own relationship with you. Amen.

DAY 27

TENDER MOMENTS: SHARE YOUR HEART

Then he saved us—not because we were good enough to be saved but because of his kindness and pity.

Titus 3:5 TLB

Unconditionally

Mom: In your own words, explain *unconditional love* to your little one. For me, I explain to my kids that it means someone loves you no matter what you do, and how bad or how many mistakes you make. The important point to emphasize is there is nothing your child can do that God won't forgive. Nothing at all. NOTHING. That's what unconditional love means. You don't have to do anything special to be loved by God. He loves us just because we exist. He forgives us and gives us blessings not because we deserve them, but because of his kindness.

Ask your child if they think God could forgive someone if they made the following mistakes (spoiler alert—the answer is always YES.)

*Broke someone else's toy by mistake (Yes, God would forgive.)

*Broke someone else's toy on purpose, because they were jealous of the friend or the toy (Yes, God would forgive.)

*Spoke mean words, and then said they were sorry (Yes, God would forgive.)

*Spoke mean words and never said they were sorry (Yes, God would forgive.)

*Stole candy (Yes, God would forgive.)

*Missed church services (Yes, God would forgive.)

*Forgot your mom's birthday (Yes, God would forgive.)

*Lied and told your mom that you didn't forget her birthday, and then lied again to say you made a card for her at school but forgot to bring it home (Yes, God would forgive.)

Feel free to point out that even though God will always forgive, the right choice in many of these examples is to still ask *the person involved* for forgiveness. Also point out that just because God will always forgive us, doesn't mean we have free range to do whatever we want. We are still accountable for our actions.

Dear God,

Through your mercy, we are loved unconditionally. You stand by us no matter what. I don't have to do *anything* to earn your love. You give it to me freely. Somehow, you can see the goodness of the Holy Spirit in me at all times. Help me to love like you. Amen.

Silent Prayer of Gratitude for Mom:

What a blessing to have your unconditional love, Lord. Do I deserve it? It's not even worth asking because I have your unconditional love, regardless. Always. Your love for me is endless. May I clearly pass on that unconditional love to my child, so they too know how much you care. Amen.

DAY 28

ASK ME MOMENTS: CAPTURING THE DAYS

See, I have today set before you life and good.

Deuteronomy 30:15 NABRE

Current Faves

My favorite toy is

_____

My favorite book is

_____

My favorite game to play [board game, video game, or outdoor game] is

_____

My favorite park or place to go is

_____

My favorite possession of all time is

_____

Dear Jesus,

Material goods can only make me happy for a little while. You make me happy forever. Amen.

Silent Prayer of Gratitude for Mom:

> God, You have set before me life and goodness. When I see life through the eyes of my child, I see happiness, and I am ever grateful. I see joy in them, with them, and around them. You have given me this, my own life, and I thank you. Sure, there are trying days, but their life with me makes me happy. Being a mom makes me happy. Thank you for this happy, lifelong gift of motherhood. Amen.

DAY 29

CRAYON MOMENTS:
GET CREATIVE

Which one of you would hand his son a stone when he asks for a loaf of bread, or a snake when he asks for a fish? If you then... know how to give good gifts to your children, how much more will your heavenly Father give good things to those who ask him.

Matthew 7:9-11 NABRE

Draw What You Hear

This time you'll both be drawing the same image simultaneously, so each of you needs to cover your drawing as much as you can while you're creating it. There isn't much room here, so you'll be working closely with each other.

Mom: You have the advantage here because you can see the instructions. If your child can read, cover up this part of the text so they can't see it. Now, tell them you're both going to draw four of the same words, and compare them at the end. Don't show each other until you're done with all the words.

Start with the word "mousse." Odds are, they will hear "moose" and draw the woodsy animal with antlers—while you're drawing the chocolate dessert (the best you can). Now say "rows." They are bound to draw the rose flower—while you draw rows, as in a chart or lined piece of paper. Now say "heel"—but you can draw either "heal" or "heel," whichever you think of when you first hear the word without seeing the spelling. Similarly, say "see"—and draw either eye, the body of water, or the letter C.

On the count of three, remove your hands and compare your drawings. How did you each interpret the words you heard? We all view the world in our own way, even when given the same reality.

96

Dear Lord,

There are times when I am misunderstood, even when I do my best to explain and be clear. Give me the patience to understand that even though it's the same world, other people live in it through their own eyes and ears, which isn't the same as living it through my eyes and ears. I know you never misunderstand me, though. I come to you tonight with an open mind, ready to receive others as they are, and not as I want them to be. Amen.

Silent Prayer of Gratitude for Mom:

Dear Jesus, I'd never give my child a stone when they asked for bread. But there are times I think I know what my child needs better than what they *think* they need. After all, I'm the adult. I've lived through years of experience and can see the big picture far better than they can. But does that mean I'm always right? Grant me the patience to listen, and hear, what my child wants. Maybe it's for a legitimate reason they haven't explained. Maybe I misunderstood their request. But of course, don't let me be a pushover. I want to give them good gifts in the right amount. Amen.

DAY 30

SILLY MOMENTS:
SHARE A LAUGH

*No, he has told you what he wants, and this is all it is: to be
fair, just, merciful, and to walk humbly with your God.*

Micah 6:8 TLB

Walk This Way

Mom: This is a game of imitating each other's silly walks. If there isn't
enough space in the bedroom to walk at least five steps side by side, go
to the hallway or try a different area. The more space, the sillier the time
you'll have together.

Start by standing side by side. One of you goes first, demonstrating a very
silly walk while taking five steps. Feel free to add sound effects. The other
person must copy the silly walk ending in the same spot. Now turn back
and together you'll take five more steps at the same time, doing that silly
walk together, side by side, ending up where you started.

Now the other person leads. They choose a different silly walk and take five steps. The other person copies, taking five steps to end up in the same spot. Now continue together, side by side, for another of those same silly five steps.

Keep going until you can't stop laughing.

If you want to make sure you settle down enough to make it easier for the bedtime transition, end with your turn, doing a quiet "shhh" tiptoe-type creep.

Some silly walks to try:

- Walking on tippy-tip toes while crouching down every other step.

- Taking very wide strides, slowly, one step at a time, while waving arms sideways like a flag in the wind.

- Bunny hops.

- Running in place and going nowhere.

- Walking like an old granny.

- Fancy model runway walk.

- Marching band high steps.

- Side steps as fast as you can.

- Penguin waddle.

- Army man crawl.

- Quiet tiptoe.

Sound effects made with each step might include:

- Boingy boingy

- Whoop-whoop

- Bizz buzz, bizz buzz

- Hee haw, hee haw

- Chicky chicky boom, chicky chicky boom

- Hi-YAH

Dear Lord,

You walk by our side, no matter how silly we may get. Thanks for the gift of laughter, and the gift of silliness, and the gift to share them with each other. I continue to be amazed at how truly blessed we are. In Jesus' name, amen.

Silent Prayer of Gratitude for Mom:

No matter how silly our days may get, thank you for walking by my side. Amen.

DAY 31

TENDER MOMENTS: SHARE YOUR HEART

First, I tell you to pray for all people. Ask God for the things people need, and be thankful to him.

1 Timothy 2:1 ICB

Goodnight and God Bless

Mom: Tonight, tell your little one you're going to think of someone – anyone dear to you for whom you would like to pray. You'll list them one at a time and say, "Goodnight and God bless," to them out loud. To warm up and encourage participation, try starting with any favorite stuffed animals, and/or pets. You can take turns, or let the person with the people in mind keep going until they are done. They are bound to think of more as the other person speaks, so keep going until you're both satisfied and content.

It will go like this:

"Goodnight and God bless Fluffy. Thanks for giving him to us."

"Goodnight and God bless all the fish in the sea. Thanks for giving them to us."

"Goodnight and God bless the birds that sing in our backyard, and the bunnies that hop around in our bushes. Thanks for giving them to us."

"Goodnight and God bless Uncle Fred. Thanks for giving him to us."

"Goodnight and God bless my friend LaVonne. Thanks for giving her to us."

"Goodnight and God bless cousin Irwin. Thanks for giving him to us."

"Goodnight and God bless our family. Thanks for giving them to us."

When you've run out of names, end with a hug and "Good night and God bless Mommy and [child's name]. Thanks for giving us each other."

Dear Jesus,

Thank you for hearing our evening prayers tonight. Thanks for interceding for us—for praying with and for us. Thanks for loving everyone and everything we called out by name, just as much as we do. Amen.

Silent Prayer of Gratitude for Mom:

Dear Jesus, Praying for others is a good feeling. It makes me feel close to them. It makes me feel close to you. It's a win-win-win. Amen.

DAY 32

ASK ME MOMENTS: CAPTURING THE DAYS

So I conclude that, first, there is nothing better for a man than to be happy and to enjoy himself as long as he can; and second, that he should eat and drink and enjoy the fruits of his labors, for these are gifts from God.

Ecclesiastes 3:12-13 TLB

Enjoying Ourselves

Mom: Let's capture some silly moments.

The funniest joke or riddle I heard is

_____

_____

_____

Someone who can always make me laugh is

_____

A funny sound I know how to make is

_____

A funny word or sound I know is

_____

The hardest I've ever worked on a craft or project is

_____

The best outcome of cooking with family was

_____

Dear God,

We know you have a sense of humor. Just look at a blobfish or a hippopotamus. Help us to see your greatness in all our joyful, fun-filled moments, because you are the One that gave them to us. Amen.

Silent Prayer of Gratitude for Mom:

Dear Lord, Family gatherings are great places to be happy, enjoy ourselves, eat and drink, and enjoy the fruits of our labor. Like Ecclesiastes 3:12-13 says, they are gifts from you. Bless our get-togethers. May we feel your light as we enjoy food, stories, and each other's company. Amen.

DAY 33

TENDER MOMENTS: SHARE YOUR HEART

My sheep hear my voice, and I know them, and they follow me.

John 10:27 NABRE

Listen to This!

Mom: For this one, you'll need your phone. Tonight, you'll capture the beauty of your child's own voice. Sure, we make videos of them every day or so and they make them of themselves. We catch them doing silly antics, ordinary actions, heartwarming acts of love, and we race to hit the red record button. We post and share the clips. We show the clips to our friends in coffee shops or to family at gatherings. Yet odds are we never watch them again because we've moved on to the next video—but that's another topic for another time.

No matter how many videos we have stored on our phones and computers, there's something about *listening* to your child that is different from watching them. Their sweet little voice, just like the rest of their bodies and minds, changes a little every day. We don't even notice or hear it. One day they have this adorable toddler voice raising their arms at you asking to be picked up, and the next day they are asking for—maybe even demanding—brand-name toys, games, and videos. They are still your cute kid, of course, but they've changed. Wouldn't it be great to capture a snapshot in time of their little voice as is it today? (Spoiler alert: Yes!)

Grab your phone. Open your text messages and type in your own phone number to send yourself a text but don't hit Send yet. Now look for the microphone icon. It might be in the same box where you enter text, or it might be an image underneath the text box. Press and hold it and you'll see the image change. It will walk you through how to create and send a voice message.

Let your child know you are asking them to leave you a message. Hit record. They can say anything they want. They can sing. They can describe the room, talk about their day, or whatever they want. Please don't give them a script. You want to capture the real them.

You can erase and re-record as many times as you like. I'll caution you to not worry or obsess about making it the perfect recording, though. The point is to capture your child in the moment, not to capture a false perfection. Saving those mistake recordings might be the ones you cherish the most.

When done, send the audio text message to yourself. You can download it onto your phone, and even save it to your computer or the cloud so when you get a new phone it's still there. Keep it and listen to it whenever you need a pick-me-up. I promise you will cherish this beautiful sound!

Dear Lord,

Let us not only listen to each other, but really *hear* each other. It's so easy to get caught up with unimportant stuff, and not really pay attention to what is going on around us, or what is important—like family and family time. And, of course, you. Amen.

Silent Prayer of Gratitude for Mom:

> Jesus, Thanks for giving us the opportunity these past few weeks to really see and hear what each other has to say. Remind us to keep listening. Amen.

DAY 34

CRAYON MOMENTS:
GET CREATIVE

Most important of all, continue to show deep love for each other.

1 Peter 4:8 TLB

Keep in Touch

Mom: In addition to crayons today, you will need:

- Paper to write a letter
- Pencil and/or pen
- Envelope (yes, get it now)
- Stamp (OK, you can get that later)

You are going to write a letter tonight and mail it the old-fashioned way. With real paper and envelope. Together, think of someone close in your heart but not close in proximity. Who would you like to get in touch with by mail? Think of someone you haven't spoken to or seen in a while. It can be a favorite teacher, helpful librarian you see a lot, friend that has moved, far-away cousin, fun auntie or uncle, godparent, grandparent, or anyone. Maybe it's a baby relative that will have to have the letter read to them, and will be a great keepsake in years to come.

Consider also having your child write a second letter; one to their future self. In that case, address and mail it directly to them, and keep it unopened for as long as you'd like—perhaps when they graduate high school? (It's not that far off, trust me!)

If your child is old enough to write legibly on their own, have them write all or part of it (depending on your level of patience right now—I know what it's like, lol. You want this to be fun, not frustrating). Have them at least sign it.

It's important to get your child's feedback not only on what to say but on how to say it. Imagine how fun it will be for the person to open and read a letter dictated by your wee one.

- Start with a greeting, then let them know the letter is from both of you, and you are sending the letter because you love and miss them or whatever the case may be.

- You can add any detail you'd like, but I suggest adding your child's age and a frame of reference, such as grade level or most recent milestone like lost a tooth, went to camp, or got a pet. Add some details about what the child is interested in the most, like horses or building blocks.

- Add some of your own personal updates. What has changed in your world since you've seen or talked to them last, that they might want to know about? It doesn't have to be a litany.

113

- Mention what you and your child enjoy doing together. Cooking? Going to the park? Watching a certain TV show? Doing this journal together?

- Perhaps you could say that if they were to visit, you'd be able to do those activities together.

- Ask them to write back to you. Who knows, you might just have started an ongoing pen pal relationship that your child will look forward to for months or years.

- Fold and place the letter in the envelope. Seal it, so there's no hemming and hawing over the next several days, as you might get tempted to edit it. Keep it as is.

- Encourage your child to draw on the back of the envelope.

Get that letter stamped and in the mail as soon as you can.

Dear Jesus,

We love our friends and family whether we talked to them yesterday or last year. You, too, love us whether we talk to you constantly, or rarely. Keep that fire burning in our hearts so we continue to walk by faith, even if it's not in words like a recited prayer, but by actions like sending letters to far-off friends. Amen.

Silent Prayer of Gratitude for Mom:

Dear God, A great way to show our family we love them is by telling them. It can be via text, mailed letter, or even in person. It might be hard to get the words out, but this week, help me let my community of *brothers and sisters* know how much they mean to me. Amen.

DAY 35

ASK ME MOMENTS: CAPTURING THE DAYS

Do not worry about tomorrow, tomorrow will take care of itself.

Matthew 6:34 NABRE

At This Closing Moment

Right now, the weather is

_____

Right now, the room of our home we are in is

_____

and the furniture around us is

_____

When we first started this journal, we thought it would be

_____

We were surprised that this journal was more

_____

Right before opening this book tonight, we were at, doing, or feeling

_____

_____

Right now, with this as the last entry, we feel

_____

_____

Dear God,

Right now, we want to thank you for giving us these special moments together. We cherish our sacred time focused on family and faith. May we continue finding time to share special *Mommy & Me* time long after this book is finished. Amen.

Silent Prayer of Gratitude for Mom:

Dear Lord, Thank you for these past five weeks days with my child. May we never forget these golden times we spent together, learning about each other, and sharing in your love. I praise you, and I thank you. Amen.

Congratulations! You've set aside and shared 35 extra-special days with your child—and God. How lucky you all are.

Where To Go From Here:

I'm so impressed with all those micro-moments you chose to spend with your little one. Can I give you a virtual hug? You will never regret a minute—or micro-moment—of that special time together, and you now have a document to savor from it. Set it aside in a safe place. It will be so fun to look at together in a few years. If you are able to print photos, take a selfie with the two of you holding the book, and tuck it in these pages so you know exactly what the two of you looked like when you filled it out. In many cases, it will be fun to see what hairstyles and clothes you had at the time.

I bet you already realize how special this bonding has been. In a few years, you'll look back and marvel at how even more amazing it really was, and how fast time flies. You might not see it right now, but you've given your growing child a Christian foundation that will hold them steady for years to come. Be proud, Mama. I'm proud of you.

Before we close, I've got some summary questions for you to fill out. Don't just think about the answers—write them down in the space provided. You will thank yourself later. Go grab a pen or crayon. I'll wait.

Now that your five weeks are over, what have you learned?

_____

_____

_____

_____

What surprised you the most?

_____

_____

_____

_____

Has any part of your life or perspective changed as a result of this devotional? If so, is it mommy related, or an overall shift?

_____

_____

_____

_____

What would you do differently if you were to start the devotional over again?

_____

_____

_____

_____

What was the best part of the past five weeks you spent together?

_____

_____

_____

_____

From here on, my hope is that you continue to share special bedtime togetherness with your child. Ideas for moving forward:

- Flip back over the devotional and read over some entries again, to see how answers may have changed in just five short weeks. Has their handprint already grown, for example?

- For sure, I recommend doing this devotional every year to see the growth and changes. Learn from me ... you'll want a new book for each year so as to not alter any of the precious artwork (or graffiti) your child may have written. I learned the hard way when my daughter went back into one of her own little notebooks and scribbled out any drawings or thoughts she thought were *too childish*. She was 5 at the time, very precocious, and drew over them. I lost the answers she gave to her favorite foods, BFFs, adorable drawings, etc. You don't want that to happen here.

- Join a "mommy & me" playgroup at your church, neighborhood, or preschool. If one doesn't exist locally or close enough to you, create one. Consider filling out this book together, as a group, during your meetings. That's an especially good idea for introverted moms that aren't good at small talk but are craving in-person connections. It's also a great idea for groups that have wider age ranges of kids that have found it hard to find a suitable playground or location that all kids agree is fun.

- From here on, think about creating your own bedtime ritual that involves prayer and activity. It can be one of these entries, or one of your own. Won't it be great to continue the precious pattern of captured micro-moments?

- Even if it's not a nightly occurrence, I hope you never stop finding micro-moments to cherish with the beautiful creature you call your child. May God bless you both.

Pressing Needs Prayers

For times when your child needs specific help, but you are at a loss for words

Blended Families: Dear Jesus, Your earthly family with Mary and Joseph was the very model for blended families. Help us to love each other like a true family should—the welcoming and unquestioning way Joseph did with you. Let us not get caught up with *who belongs to whom*, because we are all really the same family. We are all *your* family, God. You treat us all equally. Help me to follow your example and Joseph's lead. Help me to focus on seeing the good in people—*your* good in people—regardless of where they were born or live. Let me offer new family members and reluctant family members my respect, and let me pray for the grace that they offer me theirs. Amen.

See Day 20, 34

Birthday/Celebrations: Dear Lord, As we celebrate this person and special occasion, please rain down your love and bless them abundantly. Let them know how much we love them. Fill them with your peace and leave them with a song in their joyful heart. Watch over them not only today, the day the world was graced with their very essence, but every day. Amen.

See Day 22, 32

Courage: Dear Lord, I need your help. Please give me the strength to face my fears. Right now, I want to turn away from them, but I know that's not the right choice. You live in me, and your strength is infinite, so your courage and strength are mine. Remind me you are always by my side. Remind me that together we are unstoppable. May I find the courage to push through what is making me uncomfortable, anxious, and unhappy, so I come out stronger than ever. Remind me to quietly chant, "Come Holy Spirit, come" as I take that first step. I know you will be with me. Amen.

See Day 15, Philippians 4:6 TLB

Disappointment: Dear God, I need some help. I'm disappointed that results didn't turn out the way I wanted them to, or the way I thought they should. Give me strength to work through it. Open my eyes and mind to find the positive side of what happened, even though it may be hard right now. Help me understand the potential for the goodness that will come out of it, and guide me to a new path, one with even higher success and happiness. Give me the patience to understand that your ways are not always *my* ways, but that your ways are always right. In Jesus' name, amen.

See Day 13, and prayer from Day 29, Philippians 4:12 ICB

Encouragement: Dear Jesus, I know the Bible assures me that "I can do all things through Christ" (Philippians 4:13 NLT). But sometimes I'm not so sure of myself. Today, I need a little support. I'm praying to you now for some encouragement. Help me feel your strength working within me. Help me to know that with your help, there is *nothing* I can't do. Remind me that you live in me, so no matter what happens, I am not alone, and I still have value. As I turn to you in prayer, please let me feel your needed love and support. I know you answer *knee mail*.

See Day 4, 13, prayer on Day 72

Faith Boost: Dear Lord, There is an old Bible story about a nonbeliever named Saul. You wanted him to believe so much that you sent a light from heaven so strong that he was knocked over and fell down. Please let me feel that light. I know you might not send me a real lightning bolt or spotlight, but let me feel that level of faith, the kind Saul had that turned him into a faithful follower for life. I want to believe more deeply, and I am asking for help to do that. I know you'll never give up on me. Please help faith be a larger part of my and our family's lives. There are many ways we can turn to you throughout the day. We can say grace before meals, we can thank you (out loud) for even small blessings like sunshine, and we can say prayers together as a family before bed. Help us prioritize church services as a family, so we can spend more time in your house feeling your love. It doesn't have to happen all at once. We can start out small by being grateful. The more consistent we are in being thankful, the closer to you we will become. Amen.

See Day 12, 2 Corinthians 5:7, 1 Corinthians 10:24

Family Vacation/Family Time: Dear Lord, As we spend family time together, may we ask for special blessings? Please open our hearts to love one another as you love us. Let us be patient and kind to each other. Open our eyes to see each other the way you see us. May we greet each day as a chance to have fun together. Open our ears to hear your voice when we talk with each other, eager to listen to what each other has to say. Open our minds to welcome in the beauty that surrounds us, knowing you provided every piece of it—just for us. When we are tempted to quarrel, please calm our minds and close our mouths. We thank you for our family, and we bless you for giving us this special time together. Amen.

See Day 20, Titus 3:9

First Day of School: Dear Lord, Bless us as we get ready for this extra special day. When our schedule gets a little busy or rushed preparing for this momentous occasion, help calm our nerves. Remind us that there will never be another first day of school for this grade and that we should cherish it. We are growing, and that's a gift. As we get to our classroom, remind us to not leave you at the door, but to hold you close throughout the day, every day. Be with us as we find our way around the school, and meet new people. Remind us that being a good friend is how we make good friends. Watch over Mommy during the school day, and keep her company. Bring many happy surprises for both of us. Amen.

See Day 15, 33

Gratitude and Praise: Dear Jesus, I am so thankful for all you've done, for all you've given me. I've been so blessed that I admit sometimes I feel like I don't deserve it. But I do. There is nothing I must do to deserve your love or your gifts. You give them to me freely. How can I possibly say thanks? Help me express my grateful heart—not just to you, but to anyone that offers me kindness. I may be shy and saying thank you might feel uncomfortable at first, but offering gratitude allows room for more graces to come my way. So, thanks for all your gifts so far, and every blessing yet to come. Amen.

See Day 4, 5, , 1 Corinthians 10:24

Grief/Loss of Family Member: Dear God, We ask you to welcome our loved one into the light of your undying love. We thank you for wrapping them in your care. It makes us so sad to talk about it because we miss them so much already. We were so blessed to have them in our lives. Psalm 18:6 tells us that when we are in distress and cry out for help, that you will hear our voice. We call out to you today, Lord. Please hear us now, come close, and comfort us. Blanket your love over our entire household. Calm our sadness. Help us rise above our sorrow. Fill us with the never-ending peace that only you can give. Amen.

See Day 10, 15, 30, 32, John 16:22, Psalm 34:18

Grief/Loss of Pet: Dear Lord, Thank you for the gift of our pet. We loved them so much. We are so grateful you created [pet's name] and trusted us with their care. How lucky we were for them to have taught us unselfish love. They brought us joy and made us smile. We are sad that our time together has come to an end. We miss [pet's name] being with us. Help us to remember the good times we had together. Instead of being sad when we think of them, let us focus on being thankful for all those happy times we shared while we had them. With great gratitude, we return our cherished companion back to you. Amen.

See Day 10, 15, Psalm 34:18

Guidance/Wisdom: Today we pray for wisdom and guidance. Making good choices isn't always easy. There are times we need an extra hand to help us. Give us the courage to face challenges and the strength to never give up. Please give us smart minds and kind Christian hearts to make tough decisions easier. As we continue to pray, we know you hear us. Help us listen to the guidance and wisdom you offer. Show us the right path to follow. Teach us to be patient as we walk down that guided path. Thank you for always being there for us to turn to, no matter what we are facing or going through. Amen.

See Prayer for Mom Day 1, 12, Psalm 25:4-5

Illness of Loved One: Dear Lord, It's hard to find goodness in pain. We like to see people happy and healthy. It is hard to understand when they aren't, because we know you love us so much. But we know when sickness and pain happen, that we must turn it over to you to figure out and handle. Today, we pray for the healing of our loved one. Please free them from suffering and help them. Can you help us think of ways we can pitch in and help too, like doing their laundry or making them lunch? Would you remind them you are there for them and strengthen their faith so they cast every care your way? Please let them feel in their heart that you are walking beside them. Give them what they need to see you. Amen.

See James 5:16, Psalm 107:20 ICB, Jeremiah 33:6 ICB, Psalm 41:3 ICB, Job 29:24

Jealousy: Dear God, Help me to be happy with all I have, and not worry about what I may not. Open my eyes to see what others may have has nothing to do with me. What they do or have doesn't take away from my goodness, or from all I already have. Help me learn to be happy knowing I have all I need, even when I feel I don't. The true secret of being happy is knowing "I can do all things through Christ" because He gives me strength. Having or doing isn't what makes people happy. Happiness comes from within—from you. Amen.

See Day 4, Philippians 4:12-13 ICB

Loss/Failure: Dear Jesus, Our world is full of challenges and changes, and all of them are blessings in some way. Isaiah 55:8 reminds us that your thoughts and ways are different from our thoughts and ways. Sometimes you bless us by giving us gifts and sometimes you bless us by removing them. Whichever way you choose to bless us, help us trust it's in order to love you more deeply. When we have a hard time understanding and seeing the world the way you do, deepen our trust and faith in your wisdom. Nothing is permanent, other than your love. Give us the strength to see past this temporary hiccup so we can dance together again in joy. Amen.

See Prayer Day 3, Psalm 34:18, Psalm 147:3, Revelation 21:4

Moving (to new a home, school, parish, etc.): Dear Jesus, Starting anything new can be a little scary. But starting when you don't know *anyone* can be a bigger challenge. Please watch over our family in our new surroundings. Please bless this entire new adventure. Help us reach out to make new friends and do good deeds. I am going to ask a special favor about the future—please bless our soon-to-be new friends and neighbors. I pray they happily welcome and accept us for who we are. After all, we are wonderful. We are you. We are worthy of love and acceptance everywhere we go. Never let us forget that. Amen.

See Day 10, Joshua 24:15 for moving to new home, Job 31:32

New Baby (as in, not looking forward to one): Dear Jesus, I am going to be honest. A new baby in the house is going to shake up our daily lives. I am not sure how I feel about it. I mean, in the Bible, Psalms 127:3 (NLT) says, "Children are a gift from the LORD; they are a reward from him." So, the new baby must be a positive change, right? But how will our family adjust? How will it change what we do now, and how we do it? Will the baby get all the attention? Will the crying baby keep us up all night? We come to you today to ease our concerns about the new life that will be joining our family. When I am feeling anxious, let me remember that the baby is a gift and a reward. Everything else will work out. Amen.

See Day 20, John 15:12, John 13:34

Pain: Dear Jesus, We ask you to ease our pain. The pain might be physical, in our body. The pain might be mental, in our thoughts and hearts. The pain might be inflicted on someone else entirely, someone we love very much, and it hurts us to see them go through it. We realize there are times when people or stuff need to be taken away, in order for us to be given more, like the way we make more room on a bookshelf, dresser drawer, or toy chest. We might not be able to understand what is going on. We certainly don't like it—no one likes going through pain. If you cannot ease this pain, sit by our sides as we go through it. Help us trust we can work through it. You would never give us more than we can handle. Amen.

See Day 10, 12, 14

Patience: Dear God, Throughout this journal, you have increased my faith and helped me be kinder. But right now, those blessings are wearing thin. I feel irritation scratching at me. You see my frustration. It's so hard to wait for an item we want or need so badly. I need some patience, and I need it now. I know I haven't always done work 100% the right way, or on time, and yet you have been *so* patient with me. Please renew my mind and heart. Please grant me the strength to wait this out. As I take a long, deep breath, let me feel your hand on my shoulder, calming me down, and easing the angst in my heart. Amen.

See Day 9, 14, Psalm 37:7, 1 Thessalonians 5:14

Respect: Dear Lord, Help us respect each other. Respect means we admire someone for their God-given talents and achievements. Sometimes it means listening to someone older than us, like teachers and leaders, because they have special training and know more than we do. In families, it means we listen to adults, hear what they have to say, and act accordingly. After all, grown-ups know a lot more than we do because they have had more time to listen to you, Lord. They have had more practice learning right from wrong. Give us faith in each other so we can trust the other person has our best interest in mind. Amen.

See 1 Peter 5:5, Psalms 138:6, Matthew 7:12

Sadness or Depression: Dear Jesus, I need you to ease the sadness in my heart. It feels like a hole is in my chest, or a heavy rock is sitting on it. I don't want it there anymore. I want that burden lifted. I need extra comfort from you, Lord, to make it go away. I need help and strength to fully see this is a temporary feeling. Help me understand I can get out of this dark cloud, because I know you always bring the sun back after a storm. Help me turn to others, right here, like friends and family, that can help me work through my sadness and pain. Let me open up to them so they can help me, too. In Jesus' name, amen.

See Day 10, 13, 15, Isaiah 55:12, Job 29:24

Self-Confidence (Lack of): Dear God, Sometimes I feel like I am not good enough. Sometimes I feel like everyone else is better than me, or that they deserve better than what I have. Can you remind us how we are all equal in your eyes? Can you remind me that your grace and love are given to me freely, and I don't have to do anything to deserve it, or earn it? Can you remind me how awesome I am, because you dwell in me, which means I'm practically perfect? Help me look in the mirror and remind myself, proudly, that I have value. I have worth. If there are areas of my life that make me especially self-conscious, help me turn to a trusted adult who can help me work out why I feel that way, and how I can get past that uncomfortable feeling. I am a reflection of you and deserve nothing but happiness. Amen.

See Day 4, 13, Ephesians 2:8

Sibling Rivalry:

> **For child:** Dear Jesus, Help me to see my brother/sister as a blessing. They are family, and meant to be loved. Do I feel threatened by them? Do they feel threatened by me? Let me trust them. Let me want what's best for them. Ease my mind, Lord. Remind me that arguments are a choice, and I can choose to not have them. They are with me for life, so it's no use fighting all the

time. I want to get along. I want to be on their side, Lord, like you are on mine. Please bring us closer as a family, as siblings, to share in your love together. Amen.

See James 5:9, 1 Corinthians 10:24, Psalm 133:1, Ephesians 4:32

For Mom: Dear Jesus, Teach my children to be kind and patient with each other. May they dismiss envy and pride so that when they don't see eye to eye, they can control their actions and tongues. If they do disagree, help them forgive completely. Let them come to a positive resolution that serves them both. I want them to see the best in each other, to root for and protect each other, and grow together in your love. Please help me show them how to do that. Amen.

See Day 4, 20, Psalm 133:1, Proverbs 22:6, Thessalonians 5:15

Sleepovers: Dear Jesus, Sleepovers can cause anxiety in both kids and adults. Spending the night some place else can be scary, even if it's at the house of someone we know very well. Sleepover parties add a bunch of people we don't know all that well, creating the potential for silliness that can go a little overboard. Watch over everyone at the party, and keep the focus on having a fun time celebrating. Keep everyone safe and protected in your care. But also, remind us that it's okay to decide to not want to sleep over, and we don't have to give a reason why. Sometimes we just want to be home, and that's okay. Help us to grow strong enough to spend a carefree night away from home at some point, knowing we will be back home safely the very next day. In Jesus' name, amen.

See Day 22, Philippians 4:6, Isaiah 26:3-4

Thankfulness: Dear God, This is my prayer of thanks for taking care of us every single day (since I know I don't thank you enough). You have given me more than I could ever hope. Thank you for answering my needed prayers, and for answering prayers I never asked or thought I needed. I am grateful for even the smallest of blessings that I don't say *thank you* for very often. Blessings like sunshine that warms my face, rain that makes flowers grow, birds that sing, trees that make shade, all the food we eat, and the cool clothes we wear. I thank you for family and friends that make us happy and give us love. Thank you for keeping us safe and healthy on this wonderful journey you have given us, called life. Amen.

See Colossians 2:7, 1 Thessalonians 5:16-18, Hebrews 12:28-29, Psalm 69:30

Trust: Dear God, it can be hard to trust people sometimes. I know *you* never let me down. But still, sometimes when I'm hurt or afraid, it's so hard to trust you when I can't see you or talk to you face to face. Help me to trust you. Help me to get out of the way so you can make it work according to your will. I know you have the right answers. I might not be able to see why or understand your reasons yet. I need some extra faith right now. Whatever ends up happening, help me to trust it will all work out. Amen.

See Day 12, Isaiah 26:3, Philippians 4:6

Acknowledgments

I want to thank my kids Lucy, Mitch, and Vinny, who helped raise me just as much as I helped raise them. How I wish a book like this was around when you were at the age you still listened to me (hah! just kidding, kids, Momma loves you!). There are so many micro-moments with each of you that I treasure in my heart ("careful of my belly button!" "pinger" "is Bruce a real name?"), and I hope there are micro-moments with me you treasure too.

To my husband, who quickly realized we were outnumbered but always kept a level head even with the addition of ponies, cats, birds, and way too much yard to mow.

And of course, thank you Jesus, whose faithfulness in me I someday hope to deserve.

MEET THE AUTHOR

Bitsy Kemper is an award-winning author who took a delightfully unconventional path. After earning dual undergraduate degrees and an MBA, she spent too many years in corporate marketing getting interviewed on CNN, co-writing a syndicated column, and appearing in hundreds of media outlets worldwide. In her free time, she garnered public speaking accolades, starred in an award-winning local TV show, emceed events, and appeared in movies and commercials.

Eventually, Bitsy embraced her true creative calling and is now blissfully immersed in the wonderful world of authorship. With 23 published children's books under her belt, she thrills in visiting schools and libraries.

A mom of three (four if you count her husband), Bitsy understands how quickly childhood flies by. Having three kids in just over four years taught her the importance of cherishing "micro-moments." That's why she wrote this devotional - to help other moms spend more magical time with their children. Not only does this book offer a way to honor the mother-child bond, it leaves families with a cherished keepsake. Bitsy is very excited to help moms and kids nurture their relationship with each other and God. Easily. And in a fun way.

You can find out more about Bitsy at www.BitsyKemper.com.

Scripture Index
In order of appearance:

Proverbs 31:26-29 TLB

Psalm 139:4 ICB

James 1:5 Paraphrased

Isaiah 49:16,18 ICB

Esther 1:6 TLB

1 Thessalonians 5:11 TLB

Psalm 19:1 ICB

Proverbs 27:9 ICB

James 1:17 NABRE

Matthew 10:42 TLB

Psalm 52:8 ICB

Proverbs 4:23 ICB

John 13:34 NABRE

Proverbs 3:5 ICB

1 Corinthians 2:11-12 TLB

Psalm 118:24 NABRE

2 Timothy 1:7 ICB

Galatians 5:25 NABRE

Job 8:21 ICB

Isaiah 49:13 NABRE

John 9:25 NABRE

Psalm 133:1 ICB

Ecclesiastes 7:10 TLB

Ephesians 5:19 ICB

Deuteronomy 11:13 ICB

Genesis 17:7 TLB

Ecclesiastes 12:1 ICB

Psalm 139:2 NABRE

Titus 3:5 TLB

Deuteronomy 30:15 NABRE

Matthew 7:9-11 NABRE

Micah 6:8 TLB
1 Timothy 2:1 ICB
Ecclesiastes 3:12-13 TLB
John 10:27 NABRE
1 Peter 4:8 TLB
Matthew 6:34 NABRE

In ABC order:

1 Corinthians 2:11-12 TLB
1 Peter 4:8 TLB
1 Thessalonians 5:11 TLB
1 Timothy 2:1 ICB
2 Timothy 1:7 ICB
Deuteronomy 11:13 ICB
Deuteronomy 30:15 NABRE
Ecclesiastes 3:12-13 TLB
Ecclesiastes 7:10 TLB
Ecclesiastes 12:1 ICB
Ephesians 5:19 ICB
Esther 1:6 TLB
Galatians 5:25 NABRE
Genesis 17:7 TLB
Isaiah 49:13 NABRE
Isaiah 49:16,18 ICB
James 1:5 Paraphrased
James 1:17 NABRE
Job 8:21 ICB
John 9:25 NABRE
John 10:27 NABRE
John 13:34 NABRE
Matthew 6:34 NABRE
Matthew 7:9-11 NABRE
Matthew 10:42 TLB

Micah 6:8 TLB
Proverbs 3:5 ICB
Proverbs 4:23 ICB
Proverbs 27:9 ICB
Proverbs 31:26-29 TLB
Psalm 19:1 ICB
Psalm 52:8 ICB
Psalm 118:24 NABRE
Psalm 133:1 ICB
Psalm 139:2 NABRE
Psalm 139:4 ICB
Titus 3:5 TLB

Made in United States
Troutdale, OR
05/15/2024

19897403R00080